Is This Supposed To Be Funny?

Hugleikur Dagsson

Is This Supposed To Be Funny?

MICHAEL JOSEPH
an imprint of
PENGUIN BOOKS

MICHAEL JOSEPH

Published by the Penguin Group
Penguin Books Ltd, 80 Strand, London WC2R ORL, England
Penguin Group (USA) Inc., 375 Hudson Street, New York, New York 10014, USA
Penguin Group (Canada), 90 Eglinton Avenue East, Suite 700, Toronto, Ontario, Canada M4P 2Y3
(a division of Pearson Penguin Canada Inc.)
Penguin Ireland, 25 St Stephen's Green, Dublin 2, Ireland (a division of Penguin Books Ltd)
Penguin Group (Australia), 250 Camberwell Road,
Camberwell, Victoria 3124, Australia (a division of Pearson Australia Group Pty Ltd)
Penguin Books India Pvt Ltd, 11 Community Centre,
Penguin Group (NZ), 67 Apollo Drive, Mairangi Bay, Auckland 1310, New Zealand
(a division of Pearson New Zealand Ltd)
Penguin Books (South Africa) (Pty) Ltd, 24 Sturdee Avenue,
Rosebank, Johannesburg 2196, South Africa

Penguin Books Ltd, Registered Offices: 80 Strand, London WC2R ORL, England

www.penguin.com

First published as *Bjargið okkur* by JPV Publishers, Iceland 2005
Published by Michael Joseph 2007
I

Copyright © Hugleikur Dagsson, 2005

The moral right of the author has been asserted

Printed in Great Britain by Clays Ltd, St Ives plc

A CIP catalogue record for this book is available from the British Library

ISBN: 978-0-718-15343-4

Prologue

'Is this supposed to be funny?' asks Mr Dagsson's second offering to the English reader, and a valid question it is. The Icelandic public rather approves of Dagsson's numerous books, plays, musicals, comic strips, radio programmes and what not. Of course, the Icelandic public approves of a lot of things: from whale hunting and convicted criminals in the senate to the imprisonment and deportation of Falun Gong members.

Icelanders also highly appreciate the Eurovision song contest and a tradition of celebrating it has developed in the past few years, in spite of Iceland's contributions rarely making it past the semifinals into the actual competition. Iceland's largest shopping mall is accurately shaped like a phallus. From afar it looks like it was designed by a doctor, not an architect. Its opening date was 10/10/01 at 10:10. In binary code that spells the number of the beast. Dagsson usually spends his weekends there, wandering aimlessly, trembling with inspiration. This environment provides the fertile ground whereout his cartoons sprout.

I believe that the book's title refers to its morally dubious content. Within its pages are Dagsson's thoughts on the subject and a very subtle comparison to immorality's identical twin: absolute innocence. Or maybe not. Maybe this book is a product aimed at the matured Garfield reader or whatever hole in the market that demands this sort of thing. This work of Dagsson's does not in itself contribute to Western society's decaying morality, it is simply one of its manifestations. And as such, very interesting and enjoyable.

Friðrik Sólnes, electrician

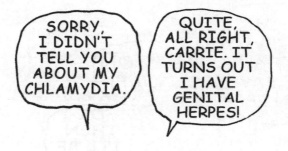

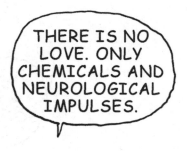

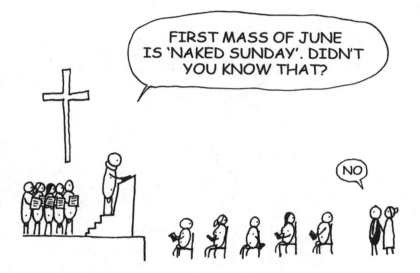

GOOD DAY TO YOU SIR. MAY I PUT UP A FEW 'GAY PRIDE' POSTERS AROUND YOUR ESTABLISHMENT?
KKK FOR EVER

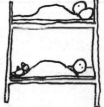

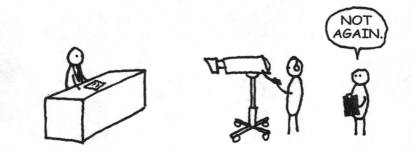

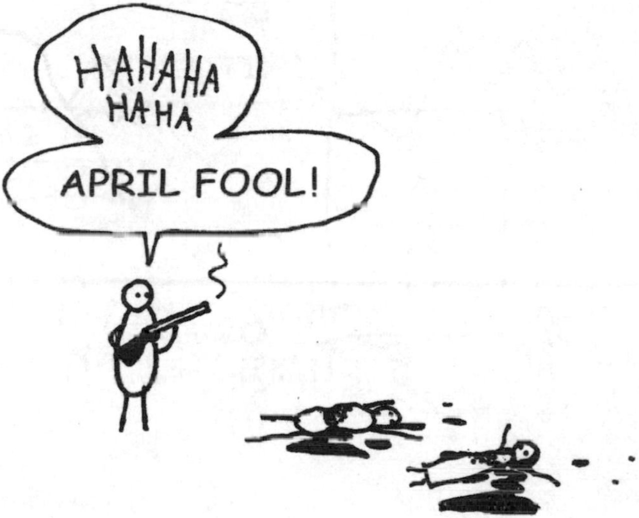
HAHAHA
HAHA
APRIL FOOL!

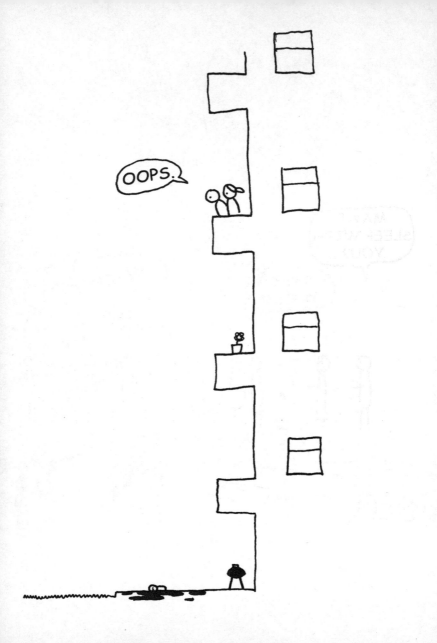

YOUR BREATH STINKS, HONEY.

OH, RIGHT. I WAS WIPING OUR LITTLE CHUCK'S ARSE. BUT THERE WAS NO TOILET PAPER, SO I USED MY TONGUE.

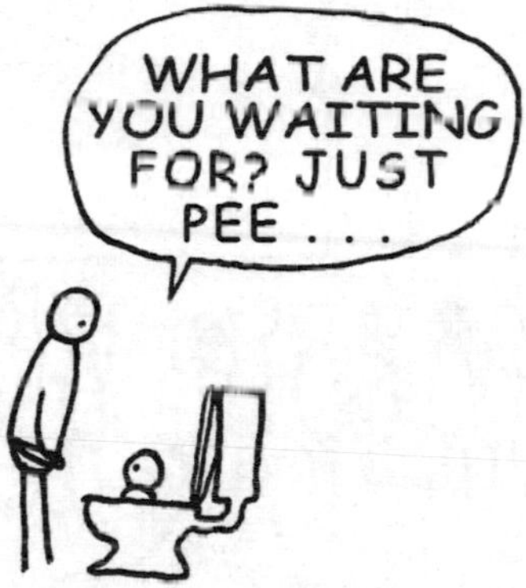
WHAT ARE YOU WAITING FOR? JUST PEE . . .

SHUT THE FUCK UP, YOU SON OF A BITCH!
THAT MAKES YOU THE BITCH, MUM.